北京
Beijing

明
MING

南京
Nanjing

Pacific Ocean

太
平
洋

昆明
Kunming

葛剌
al

浙地港
Chittagong

占城
Champa

暹羅
Siam

真臘
Cambodia

a

南渤里
Lambri

苏門荅臘
Sumatra

滿剌加
Malacca

Borneo
渤泥

舊港
Palembang

Java 爪哇

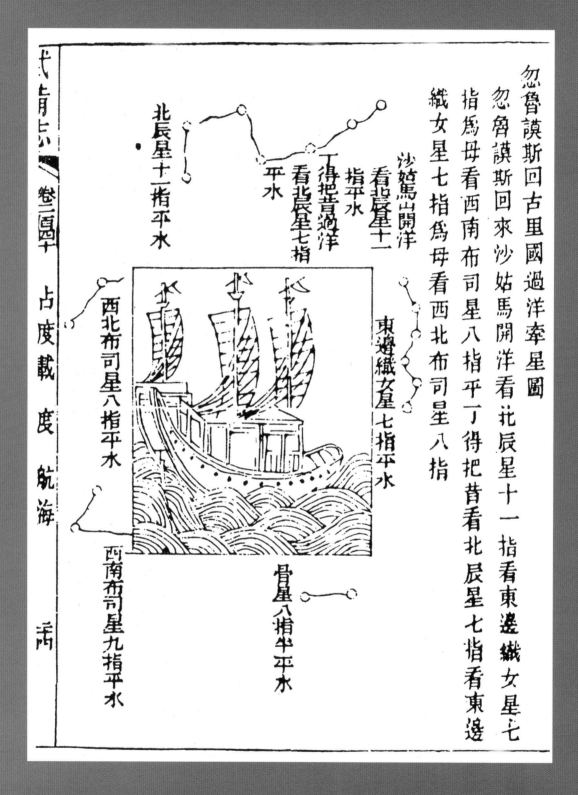

忽魯謨斯回古里國過洋牽星圖

忽魯謨斯回來沙姑馬開洋看北辰星十一指看東邊織女星七

指為母看西南布司星八指平丁得把昔看北辰星七指看東邊

織女星七指為母看西北布司星八指

沙姑馬山開洋
看北辰星十一
指平水

丁得把昔過洋
看北辰星七指

北辰星十一指平水

東邊織女星七指平水

西北布司星八指平水

西南布司星九指平水

骨星八指半平水

The Great Voyages
OF
Zheng He

Published in the United States of America by
Pan Asian Publications (USA) Inc.
29564 Union City Boulevard, Union City, CA 94587
Tel. (510) 475-1185 Fax (510) 475-1489

Published in Canada by
Pan Asian Publications Inc.
110 Silver Star Boulevard, Unit 109
Scarborough, Ontario M1V 5A2

ISBN 1-57227-088-8
Library of Congress Control Number: 2005924226

Book design and layout by Lorna Mulligan
Art reproduction and transparencies by Michel Filion Photography

Printed in Taiwan

The Great Voyages
OF
Zheng He

Text by Song Nan Zhang & Hao Yu Zhang
Illustrated by Song Nan Zhang

Pan Asian Publications

IT WAS THE BEGINNING of the monsoon season nearly 600 years ago in southern China, and the frequent northeastern winds were ideal for sailing. At the mouth of the Yangtze River, the biggest naval fleet the world had ever seen was ready to launch an epic voyage. With hundreds of ships, some measuring over 400 feet long, this magnificent Chinese armada set sail from the Pacific Ocean toward the Indian Ocean.

In addition to senior Ming dynasty dignitaries, on board the ships were numerous technicians, navigators, doctors, meteorologists, chefs, support crews, and more than 20,000 sailors. The first stop was to be along the coastline of Southeast Asia.

At the core of the fleet were 62 "treasure" ships, escorted by 225 freight and combat junks, loaded with the finest silks, brocades, teas, porcelains, arts, and special merchandise. The freight ships carried everything from food, water, and medicines to weapons and ammunitions.

Under the command of Imperial Admiral *Zheng He*, the impressive maritime parade showcased China's daring exploration, national wealth, and military might in the 15th century.

This is the story of *Zheng He,* the commander of the fleet.

ZHENG HE WAS ONE OF six children born to devout Muslim parents living in Kunming, Yunnan, in 1371. As a young boy he was told that his ancestors had originated from the Kingdom of Bukhara. During the Yuan dynasty his great-great-great grandfather had fought alongside the Mongol ruler, Genghis Khan, and was awarded the honorable governorship of the province of Yunnan. There, the family gradually settled and flourished in the capital city of Kunming. The Chinese surname of *Ma,* which is short for Mohammad, was adopted and *Zheng He* was born as *Ma He.*

In his growing years, *Ma He* was fascinated by his father's pilgrimage to the holy land of Mecca, and dreamed about the day when he would be able to follow his footsteps. *Ma He* was taught in Chinese and Arabic and was well read in the literature of both cultures. The adventures of the Arabian folk hero, Sinbad, were among his favorite stories and they inspired a powerful sense of curiosity and imagination in him.

 I N 1381 AT THE AGE OF TEN, *Ma He*'s world was turned upside down.

After years of civil war, the once dominant Mongol power of Yuan collapsed under continual Chinese peasant uprisings. The next year, the new power of Ming invaded *Ma He*'s hometown, executed the adults, and kidnapped the youngsters from prominent families. *Ma He* was brought to the palace and forced to serve as a eunuch.

Despite that horrid event, *Ma He* transformed his misfortune into courage. He was sent to Beijing and became the trusted attendant of Prince *Zhu Di*. *Ma He* distinguished himself as a diligent student in all subject areas and skills. He demonstrated loyalty and bravery toward his master, and soon proved himself to be *Zhu Di*'s indispensable right-hand man, thriving in military planning and strategies.

When *Ma He* turned 31 in 1402, *Zhu Di* defeated all of his rival siblings and became the new Emperor of Ming. In appreciation of *Ma He*'s faithful dedication to his master, Emperor *Zhu Di* granted him wealth, title, and a noble family name. *Ma He* became known as *Zheng He*.

BEING THE THIRD EMPEROR of the Ming dynasty, *Zhu Di* was a capable and ambitious administrator. He visualized Ming as an empire more powerful and more prosperous than his predecessors in the Han and the Tang dynasties. He engaged himself in major reconstruction projects in the country. By strengthening the Great Wall, building the Grand Canal, stimulating the economy, and fending off the Mongol remnants, *Zhu Di* slowly but surely energized China into a political superpower.

All of that was not enough. The new Ming emperor tried to legitimize his reign by gaining recognition from the outside world. To entice foreign countries to pay tribute to the new China, *Zhu Di* officiated over the building of the largest navy in the world to carry out his ambition.

Knowledgeable in warfare and diplomacy along with being cultured in the arts and religion, *Zheng He,* being a man of integrity, was the perfect choice to lead such a massive nautical undertaking. When he took on the challenge and set out for his first voyage, *Zheng He* was only 32 years of age.

NO ONE KNEW BETTER than *Zheng He* the scope of this seafaring operation. It took him more than two years to get ready. With the authority given to him, *Zheng He* was able to summon the manpower and the resources necessary to form a naval force that superseded all others in recorded history.

The centerpiece of this advanced fleet was a group of 62 treasure ships that transported goods for trading purposes. A typical treasure ship measured up to 138 meters (453 feet) long and 56 meters (184 feet) wide. It had up to nine masts with 12 sails and could carry 1,500 tons of cargo. In addition to small boats that fostered communications among the ships, surrounding the cargo ships were battle ships to mobilize the sailors, supply ships to house animals and maintenance needs, and food and water ships to accommodate daily food supplies.

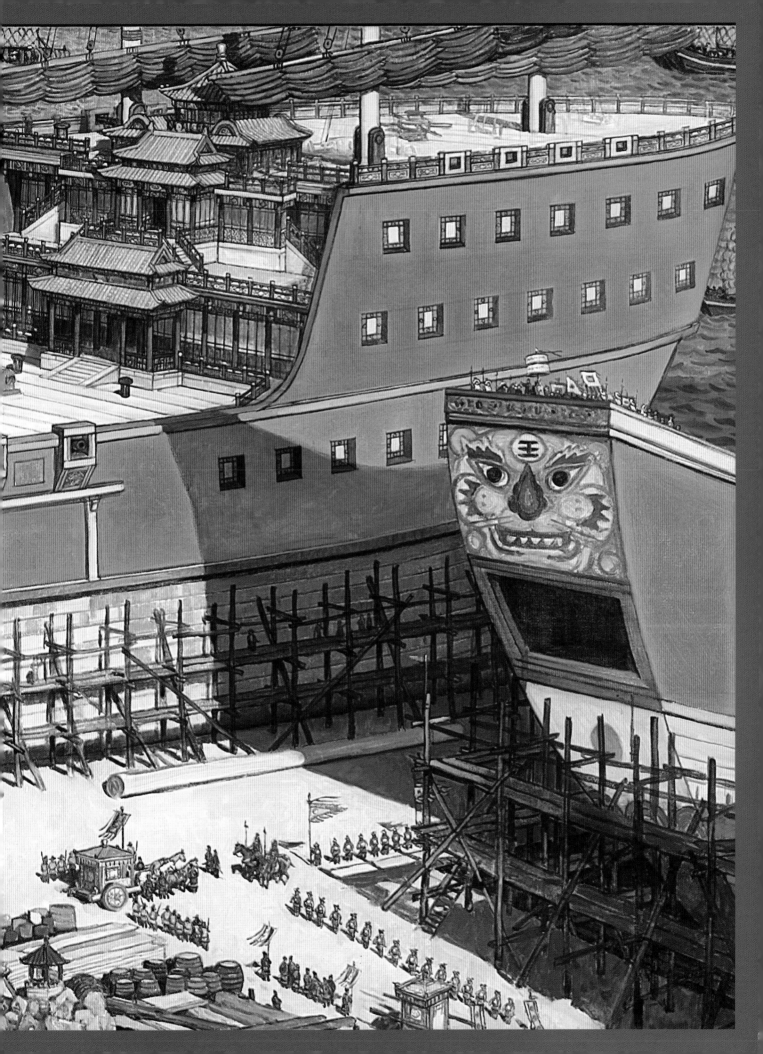

AT FIRST *ZHENG HE* took short journeys to Japan and Thailand to test run his program and train his sailors. Equipped with improved compasses, newly fashioned maps, and a fledgling knowledge of astronomy, *Zheng He*'s premier team of navigation experts were believed to be among the first in the world to sail far into the ocean and come back safely.

The ability to reliably calculate a ship's movement and direction on the vast ocean surface set the Chinese navy apart and above others in the world. The ships could chart and follow a predetermined route into the sea instead of trailing along the coastlines where there was the constant danger of capsizing or being shipwrecked.

Now, *Zheng He* was truly ready.

IN HIS FIRST VOYAGE in 1405, *Zheng He* dropped anchor in Champa (Vietnam), Java, Sumatra, Malacca, Ceylon (Sri Lanka), and even the ancient port of Calicut, India. He reached out to the people and the governments everywhere he visited. It was an understatement to describe the reaction of the people to the riches and sophistication of the Ming fleet as astonishing. As a result, the rulers of every country yearned to establish diplomatic relations with China.

Calicut, already a busy commercial port along the Indian Ocean, welcomed the sudden surge of excitement brought on by *Zheng He* and his vessels. The streets and markets were crowded with merchants from as far away as Europe and Arabia. The leader of the city, Shah Le Miti, eagerly saluted *Zheng He* and his entourage. In exchange for his goodwill, *Zheng He* gifted the Shah lavishly with an array of treasures, and he made a record-breaking business transaction with the people of Calicut that shocked this part of the world at that time.

Today, in the center of Calicut stands an epitaph written in Chinese chronicling that historic event.

ON THE WAY HOME, *Zheng He* and his ships docked in Palembang, southeast of Sumatra on the western end of the Straight of Malacca. This area was a popular passage for commercial and private ships; and consequently, a constant temptation to the preying pirates.

Zheng He's fleet did not escape the attention of one such pirate, *Chen Zuyi,* also a Chinese. As a disguise, *Chen Zuyi* and his men surrendered to the dominion of Ming, and secretly plotted an ambush to take control. He was, however, exposed and his plans failed. In a well documented, sweeping sea battle, the pirate ships were wiped out while *Chen Zuyi* was captured, and his cohorts killed.

Zheng He's success in restoring sea safety earned him widespread reputation in the region. By 1407, nearly two years after they left China, the fleet arrived home. Emperor *Zhu Di* was so overjoyed in receiving grateful foreign diplomats and emissaries that he generously rewarded each and every participant in the voyage. After a brief layover and a hectic ship maintenance schedule, *Zheng He* took on new missions and embarked on his next voyage.

ACCOMPANIED BY ACADEMIA and scholars on each of *Zheng He*'s voyages, there was no shortage of cultural exchange with the groups of people they encountered. *Zheng He* faithfully kept track of the details of the people and places, their geography and history, their belief systems and customs. These records proved to be valuable and essential in the future study of cultural anthropology.

The meteorologists and navigators on board contributed to collecting data on climate changes and weather patterns, mapping shallow spots, and charting unknown waters. All in all, this first-hand and comprehensive navigation program became one of the proud legacies of China.

Zheng He also developed a keen interest in the plants and animals from the exotic lands. He ordered them to be carefully gathered and cataloged for various occasions and purposes. Some of these unusual natural resources, such as bird nests from Borneo and aloeswood from Malacca, had been so well adopted by the Chinese that they became national delights.

THE KING OF CEYLON was the only foreign ruler that challenged the Ming fleet. He not only delayed his meeting with *Zheng He,* he even staged raids against the whole fleet. Ceylon was strategically located between China and the Arabic and African countries. It was once the holy place of Buddha where believers paid their homage.

On each of his voyages, *Zheng He* would worship at the Buddhist temples in Ceylon and make generous offerings to the monks. Yet, his good wishes fell on deaf ears. On *Zheng He*'s third visit, the King of Ceylon refused to reciprocate. He dispatched soldiers to attack the fleet while *Zheng He* was trapped and isolated. The experienced admiral did not panic. Instead, he fought straight to the palace and captured the chieftain and his family in a special operation. After that, the King of Ceylon accepted a treaty to pay tribute to China.

THE POLITICAL STABILITY between China and Ceylon exemplified the role *Zheng He* and his men played on the oceans. Peace was often restored and trade routes secured for all. On the fourth voyage, the fleet was finally able to reach its long-awaited destination of Arabia.

Similar to the Chinese, the Arabs enjoyed a rich tradition of culture, commerce, and marine history. It was a tremendous privilege for *Zheng He* to personally share his family heritage and religious beliefs with the people whom he had pictured in his mind to meet all these years. Naturally, he was warmly received at every port of call.

Not unlike other journeys, *Zheng He* successfully traded with local merchants. The Strait of Hormuz, the hub of international trade by the Persian Gulf, was one of his favorite stops. *Zheng He* bartered countless Chinese goods for special items from Arabia and Africa. Among those inventoried were gems and stones, spices, rhino horns and ivory, pearls and rouges, stallions and daggers.

IN ORDER TO VISIT more areas, the fleet was divided into smaller groups and this facilitated more discoveries. Djofar, Aden, Mecca in Arabia; and Mogadishu, Brava, and Malindi in East Africa, just to name a few, were among the expeditions.

One of the gifts from the ruler of Malindi was a full-grown giraffe. Chinese equated the animal to *qilin,* the legendary creature that would appear only when a country was governed well and its people content. When the dark-skinned Africans paraded this *qilin* on Chinese soil, they became instant celebrities. People crowded along the main streets in the capital city just to catch a glimpse of the newcomers. Best of all, Emperor *Zhu Di* was whole-heartedly praised by his subjects, and his legitimacy was no longer questioned.

More unique animals were introduced to China during *Zheng He*'s fifth voyage. Emperor *Zhu Di* ordered the construction of an imperial garden to house all the extraordinary looking animals. This became the very first zoo in China.

ZHENG HE SET OFF on his sixth voyage in 1421. Part of the mission's objective was to escort foreign dignitaries on the return to their homelands. To efficiently accomplish this goal, *Zheng He* designated four different routes among the ships in order to make more than 30 stops. His team returned to China shortly after a year, but it took three more years before all the other ships returned.

At the height of navigational breakthroughs, favorable diplomacy, and growing international trade, Emperor *Zhu Di* passed away during a lingering war with the Mongols. His son took over the throne, and all of a sudden, China was left in political and economic chaos.

That event offered the opposing party a perfect opportunity to voice their concerns. Over the years, the extravagant operation of keeping an overwhelming fleet had cost the country dearly. The new emperor was persuaded to completely ban new voyages and related activities. *Zheng He* and his men were stripped of their jobs. The great ships, now considered frivolous, were left to rot at their moorings and the records of their journeys were destroyed. The true distances these Chinese ships had reached were forever lost.

AFTER ONLY A FEW YEARS, *Zhu Di's* son became ill and his grandson came to power in 1431. Contrary to the popular self-imposed isolation ideal, the new emperor longed for the worldwide adoration and applause of the bygone years. He approached *Zheng He* to go out to sea for a seventh time.

Now in his 60s, *Zheng He* respectfully took on the responsibility of rebuilding the fleet. At the temple by the harbor where he would embark, *Zheng He* reverently sought protection from the spirits. Monuments were erected to recount his previous voyages in broad strokes. Fate would have it, however, that this would be the last of his expeditions.

On the returning leg of the campaign in 1433, *Zheng He* passed away at the age of 62, and his beloved sailors bid him a solemn farewell. There was no one before him or after him who had the knowledge or the skills to move China forward and outward into the world by sea. More than half a century later, Columbus "discovered" America, Vasco da Gama rounded the Cape of Good Hope, Magellan cruised around the globe, and all the accolade went to those European explorers.

Bibliography

鄭和下西洋：1421中國發現世界 (日)上杉千年著 上海社會科學院出版社 2003年

中西文化交流史 p.302-309, 345-348 沈福偉著 上海人民出版社 1985年

鄭和 (上、下卷) 朱蘇進、陳敏莉著 江蘇文藝出版社 2003年

一個宦官的傳奇歷程 - 鄭和的一生 石山著 遠流出版社 2000年

海上第一人：鄭和 (上、下卷) 王佩云著 實學社 2003年

中國發現世界 (英)孟西士著 遠流出版社 2003年

傑出航海家鄭和 - 鄭和下西洋的歷史研究 陳水源著 晨星出版社 2000年

中華文明大博覽(下卷) p.1398-1399 廣東旅遊出版社 1997年

圖說中華五千年(下冊) p.215-217 三聯書店(香港)有限公司 1992年

China: Cambridge Illustrated History p.209-211 Cambridge University Press 1996

Ancient China (Eyewitness Books) p.60-61 Dorling Kindersley Ltd., 1994

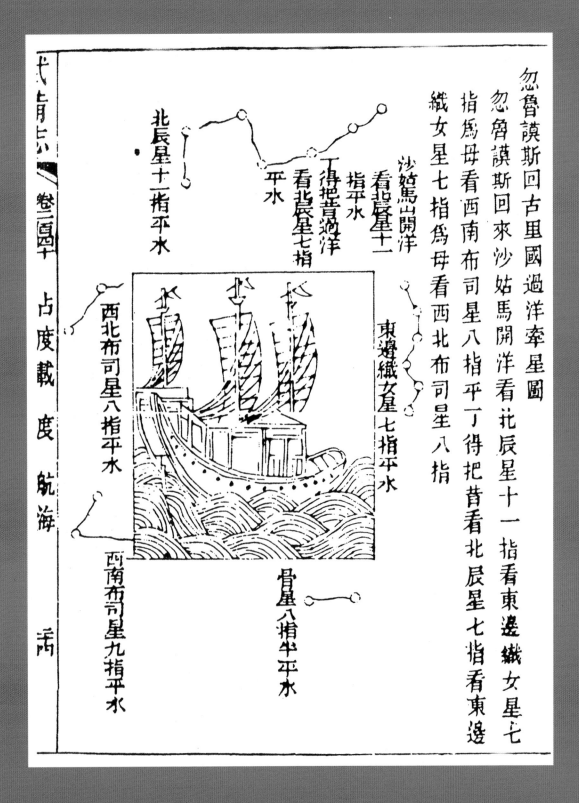

忽魯謨斯回古里國過洋牽星圖

忽魯謨斯回來沙姑馬開洋看北辰星十一指看東邊織女星七

指為母看西南布司星八指平丁得把昔看北辰星七指看東邊

織女星七指為母看西北布司星八指

沙姑馬山開洋

看北辰星十一

指平水

丁得把昔過洋

看北辰星七指

平水

北辰星十一指平水

東邊織女星七指平水

西北布司星八指平水

西南布司星九指平水

骨星八指半平水

布哈剌
Bukhara

INDIA
印 度

忽鲁谟斯
Hormuz

天方
Mecca

祖法兒
Djofar

阿丹
Aden

古里
Calicut

柯枝
Cochin

AFRICA
非 洲

Sri

Indian Ocean
印 度 洋

木骨都束
不剌哇
Mogadishu

Brava

麻林
Malindi

鄭 和 下 西 洋 航 線 圖
The Map of Great Voyages of Zheng He